Rebecca Manley Pippert

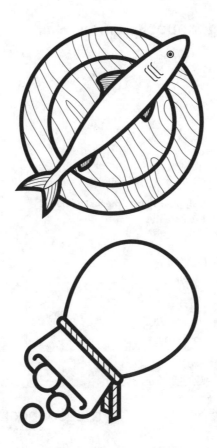

Six encounters with Jesus
from the Gospel of Luke

thegoodbook
COMPANY

Read Becky's comments on each
of the questions at:

thegoodbook.com/uncoveringlifeguide

Uncovering the Life of Jesus
© Rebecca Manley Pippert 2015. Reprinted 2016, 2017.

**This material was previously published as the first edition of
UNCOVER LUKE seeker Bible studies**

Published by
The Good Book Company
Tel (UK): 0333 123 0880
Tel (US): 866 244 2165
International: +44 (0) 208 942 0880
Email (UK): info@thegoodbook.co.uk
Email (US): info@thegoodbook.com

Websites:
North America: www.thegoodbook.com
UK: www.thegoodbook.co.uk
Australia: www.thegoodbook.com.au
New Zealand: www.thegoodbook.co.nz

ISBN: 9781910307632

Printed in Turkey
Design by André Parker

Contents

INTRODUCTION

Uncover, investigate, and examine the evidence...

People have two things in common: we want to be happy and we want to be loved. Why are these simple desires so difficult to satisfy?

Part of the ache comes from our sense that there seems to be something more promised. There is more for us to live for, to embrace, or be embraced by. We want to know that our lives are significant.

How can we discover and live with a deeper sense of life's meaning? When I was an agnostic I investigated various religions, until one day it occurred to me that I had never read the Bible. I realized that for the sake of intellectual integrity I couldn't reject something that I had never examined. I had to investigate the evidence and scrutinize the claims Jesus made about himself.

I vividly remember the first time I read one of the Gospel accounts that tell the story of Jesus. My impression of Jesus had been that he was probably sincere, and no doubt always blissfully happy. Then I started reading the Bible. I was not prepared for how much of what I discovered would challenge my pre-conceived ideas.

Here was Jesus: amazingly attractive, yet utterly exasperating. He claimed to be the Prince of Peace, yet he threw furniture down the front steps of the temple. He claimed to be the Son of God, yet one of the chief complaints about him was that he wasn't religious enough! This was not the kind of Jesus I had expected to encounter.

Maybe you've never read the Bible before. Or perhaps you've never looked at the life of Jesus with a critical mind. Whatever your story, one thing is certain: it's impossible to make an informed decision without first investigating the evidence This guide is for anyone who is genuinely seeking; who has honest questions and who wants to find out about the real Jesus. It is not necessary to believe in Jesus or accept the Bible as "divinely inspired" to use it. Rather, come to the accounts of Jesus as you would to any other historical document, with an open mind and heart, and see what you find.

Becky

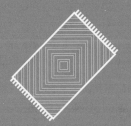

1

LUKE 1 v 1-4 & 5 v 17-26

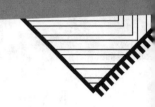

Standing Room Only

Question

Have you ever heard a friend say something like: *"If only I could get my deepest wish fulfilled, then I would be happy"*?

How true do you think that statement is and why?

Historical context

Jesus was extremely controversial in his day. While the common, despised or marginalized people were drawn to him, the religious authorities were frequently incensed by his claims, his associations and his lifestyle.

There were several types of religious leaders in Jesus' day. In this story we are introduced to two significant groups. The Pharisees were a religious sect of Jews who focused on a strict interpretation of the Law of Moses (the first five books of the Bible). The second group, called the teachers of the law (some of whom were also Pharisees), were professionally trained in teaching and applying the law.

We will meet a paralyzed man and his faithful friends, who were so eager for him to be healed of paralysis that they went to where Jesus was teaching in a Galilean town. To their surprise the house was packed not only with local people, but with religious leaders who had traveled from all over the country to listen to this new rabbi who was gaining so much attention. We never learn the paralyzed man's name nor how he developed this condition. Jesus responds to his need in a surprising way.

Many have undertaken to draw up an account of the things that have been fulfilled among us, ² just as they were handed down to us by those who from the first were eyewitnesses and servants of the word. ³ With this in mind, since I myself have carefully investigated everything from the beginning, I too decided to write an orderly account for you, most excellent Theophilus, ⁴ so that you may know the certainty of the things you have been taught.

Note: The small numbers in the Bible passages refer to the numbers of the verses.

1 What was Luke's method in writing and what was his purpose (v 3-4)?

One day Jesus was teaching, and Pharisees and teachers of the law were sitting there. They had come from every village of Galilee and from Judea and Jerusalem. And the power of the Lord was with Jesus to heal the sick. ¹⁸ Some men came carrying a paralyzed man on a mat and tried to take him into the house to lay him before Jesus. ¹⁹ When they could not find a way to do this because of the crowd, they went up on the roof and lowered him on his mat through the tiles into the middle of the crowd, right in front of Jesus.

²⁰ When Jesus saw their faith, he said, "Friend, your sins are forgiven."

²¹ The Pharisees and the teachers of the law began thinking to themselves, "Who is this fellow who speaks blasphemy? Who can forgive sins but God alone?"

²² Jesus knew what they were thinking and asked, "Why are you thinking these things in your hearts? ²³ Which is easier: to say, 'Your sins are forgiven,' or to say, 'Get up and walk'? ²⁴ But I want

you to know that the Son of Man has authority on earth to forgive sins." So he said to the paralyzed man, "I tell you, get up, take your mat and go home." ²⁵ Immediately he stood up in front of them, took what he had been lying on and went home praising God. ²⁶ Everyone was amazed and gave praise to God. They were filled with awe and said, "We have seen remarkable things today."

Jesus is teaching in the region of the Galilee. The distance from Jerusalem (in the south) to the town of Capernaum (in the north where Jesus was based) is 120 miles. It would take a fit person four or five days to walk that distance!

② Note where these religious authorities came from (v 17). Why do you think some of the Pharisees and teachers of the law decided to travel such distances and all at the same time?

③ Describe what life would be like for someone paralyzed: both practically and emotionally.

④ Once the men realize they can't get through the door because of the crowd, what alternative plan do they devise and what are the risks involved (v 18-19)?

⑤ Clearly this dramatic event would affect people in different ways. Try to imagine the reaction of those present to what they saw happening: The religious authorities and townspeople? The owners of the home? Jesus?

⑥ What does it say about the paralyzed man and his friends that they were so determined to get to Jesus?

⑦ What does Jesus see in these men that impresses him (v 20a)?

⑧ When Jesus says the man's sins are forgiven (v 20b), what do you think the reaction of the paralyzed man and his friends might have been?

⑨ Jesus seems to be saying to this man: "If all I do is heal your body, the happiness won't last, because the root of your problem is deeper than your physical condition." What do you think about this?

⑩ By saying that his sins were forgiven, what did these religious leaders correctly perceive about the controversial claim Jesus was indirectly making (v 21)?

The religious leaders were amazed by Jesus' healing ministry. But they were outraged by his claim to forgive sin, because they knew that was something only God could do. Jesus didn't say to the paralyzed man: "Look, we all blow it. Nobody's perfect, so just take heart in that." Instead, Jesus proclaimed that the sins of the paralyzed man were forgiven, simply because he had pronounced it so! It was an earth-shattering statement that reflected Jesus' identity and mission—which wasn't lost on the Pharisees!

But what Jesus does next shocks them even more. When the Old Testament religious leaders wanted to invoke authority, they would always cite divine (never personal) authority by saying: "Thus says the Lord." The religious leaders believed the worst sin of all was to commit blasphemy—the claim to be God.

11 What authority did Jesus invoke when he spoke to the paralyzed man (v 24b)?

Just to be absolutely certain everyone understood, what did Jesus say his healing of the paralyzed man confirmed (v 24a)?

12 Describe the scene when the paralyzed man responds to Jesus' impossible command (v 25-26).

So, why does this matter?

C. S. Lewis, an Oxford professor and Christian writer who was once a fervent atheist, wrote:

> "Then comes the real shock. Among the Jews there suddenly turns up a man who goes about talking as if he was God. He claims to forgive sins. He says he always existed. He says he is coming to judge the world at the end of time ... and when you have grasped that, you will see that what this man said was, quite simply, the most shocking thing that has ever been uttered by human lips."

Why do you think people who reject the controversial claims that Jesus made about his own identity still call him a great teacher and leader?

Notes

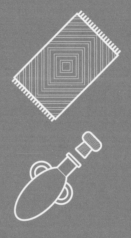

2

Guess Who's Coming to Dinner?

LUKE 7 v 36-50

Guess Who's Coming to Dinner?

Question

Why do religious people sometimes make other people feel uncomfortable?

Historical context

The Earl of Chesterfield once said that you tend to "take the tone of the company you are in." In other words, the best class of people should hang out with only the best class of people. Right? But Jesus always surprised normal society by upsetting social expectations. He made "outsiders" feel welcomed in his presence, while "insiders" were often left outraged by the company he kept.

The setting of this story is the house of a wealthy Pharisee. Sometimes for a special dinner with special guests they set up furniture in the courtyard. Uninvited people could come and stand around the sides of the courtyard and watch and listen, but they were not invited to eat. Jesus has been invited as a guest of honor in the home of Simon—a respected leader of the Pharisees. What is puzzling is why Simon goes out of his way to dishonor Jesus as his invited guest. To make matters worse, a town prostitute arrives and violates every social and religious taboo.

The story assumes that this woman had previously heard Jesus proclaiming his message of grace that God loves and forgives sinners. The Pharisees did not agree with Jesus' message, because in their view God only cared for the righteous who obeyed the law—not for law-breakers like this woman.

17

When one of the Pharisees invited Jesus to have dinner with him, he went to the Pharisee's house and reclined at the table. [37] A woman in that town who lived a sinful life learned that Jesus was eating at the Pharisee's house, so she came there with an alabaster jar of perfume. [38] As she stood behind him at his feet weeping, she began to wet his feet with her tears. Then she wiped them with her hair, kissed them and poured perfume on them.

[39] When the Pharisee who had invited him saw this, he said to himself, "If this man were a prophet, he would know who is touching him and what kind of woman she is—that she is a sinner."

[40] Jesus answered him, "Simon, I have something to tell you."

"Tell me, teacher," he said.

[41] "Two people owed money to a certain moneylender. One owed him five hundred denarii, and the other fifty. [42] Neither of them had the money to pay him back, so he forgave the debts of both. Now which of them will love him more?"

[43] Simon replied, "I suppose the one who had the bigger debt forgiven."

"You have judged correctly," Jesus said.

[44] Then he turned toward the woman and said to Simon, "Do you see this woman? I came into your house. You did not give me any water for my feet, but she wet my feet with her tears and wiped them with her hair. [45] You did not give me a kiss, but this woman, from the time I entered, has not stopped kissing my feet. [46] You did not put oil on my head, but she has poured perfume on my feet. [47] Therefore, I tell you, her many sins have been forgiven—as her great love has shown. But whoever has been forgiven little loves little."

[48] Then Jesus said to her, "Your sins are forgiven."

[49] The other guests began to say among themselves, "Who is this who even forgives sins?"

[50] Jesus said to the woman, "Your faith has saved you; go in peace."

1 In Middle-Eastern culture, hospitality is of utmost importance. What three important courtesies does Simon intentionally refuse to give Jesus (v 44-46)? In light of the Pharisees' increasingly constant complaints against Jesus, what might be Simon's motivation for inviting Jesus to this dinner?

All of the assembled guests knew that Jesus had been snubbed and deliberately insulted—but the tension is heightened because a prostitute arrives from their town. To understand this woman, we need to jump ahead to verse 47, where Jesus says: "Her many sins have been forgiven"—signifying it's a past action that has occurred already. This means she has already heard Jesus' teaching on grace and forgiveness, and has accepted it for herself (as her dramatic response to Jesus reveals).

2 Since townspeople usually assembled before the guests arrived, what might have provoked her tears as she saw Simon greet Jesus? List the things that she does (v 38). What may have motivated these actions?

3 If she knew that Jesus was to be the invited guest for the dinner, why do you think she brought her only valuable asset—an alabaster flask of expensive perfume?

4 In anointing Jesus' feet, she uses something which she may not have been able to afford to replace, and had likely used in her trade. What does her choice signify?

Jesus knew that to be touched by any woman in public—and even worse, a well-known prostitute who lowered her hair in public (a shocking offence of immodesty in that culture)—would shatter his reputation before these religious leaders.

5 Why doesn't Jesus stop her or ask her to express her gratitude in a more socially correct way?

6 What does Simon conclude about this woman, and consequently, about Jesus (v 39)?

Now Jesus takes charge and tells a story of one debtor who owed the equivalent of two years' salary to the creditor (presumably God), while the other debtor owed the equivalent of two months' salary. Simon looks at this woman and sees only her sins, but Jesus shifts the emphasis entirely in this parable.

7 How does Jesus explain this woman's extravagant actions? What do her actions reveal about what has happened in her life because of encountering Jesus (v 44-47)?

8 What does Jesus want Simon to conclude about this woman, about himself (Simon) and about God?

9 Jesus was showing Simon that her extravagant gestures of love hadn't earned her forgiveness but were the result of it. If faith, love and gratitude to God for his forgiveness, and compassion toward others, are the evidence of one's spiritual state, then how does Simon measure up?

10 How do the other guests react when Jesus declares that the woman's sins are forgiven (v 49)?

11 What effect would it have on this woman and her place in that community that Jesus publicly declared her sins forgiven (v 50)?

12 This woman has not spoken a single word, yet Jesus commends the power of her faith! How does she express her faith?

13 Simon's supreme confidence is derived from believing he is a good man who follows the rules. But what, according to Jesus, do law-keepers and law-breakers have in common? In what way is Simon more lost than this woman?

So, what might this mean for us?

This woman had profound regrets. Which of us doesn't have things we deeply regret and wish we could go back and change? But she learned from Jesus that all who recognize their sins and confess them to God can be forgiven.

If someone said to you: "I couldn't go to God, not after all I have done," how would you answer that person in light of this passage?

Notes

3

You Can Go Home Again!

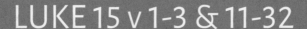
You Can Go Home Again!

Question

What might someone mean by saying they're lost?

Losing stuff and being lost are things we have all experienced in daily life. Sometimes, however, people describe themselves as feeling "lost" in a more all-encompassing sense.

Historical context

The religious leaders are again complaining that Jesus is associating with riff-raff and sinners (15 v 2). Upon hearing their complaint, Jesus addresses their concerns through three parables. We will focus on the last parable, about the love of a father for his two sons. As you read this parable, notice how Jesus deliberately pushes every orthodox-Jewish button.

It's helpful to know that in Jesus' day an inheritance was given to sons after the death of the father. The younger son's share would be one third, and the older son's share two thirds, of the father's wealth (Deuteronomy 21 v 17). Furthermore, Jewish children were raised to deeply revere their parents, obey the law and stay close as a family unit. It is hard to overestimate how shocking this parable would have been for an orthodox, conservative crowd.

Now the tax collectors and sinners were all gathering around to hear Jesus. ² But the Pharisees and the teachers of the law muttered, "This man welcomes sinners and eats with them."

³ Then Jesus told them this parable...

1 Describe the groups that Jesus was addressing and the complaints some of them were registering (v 1-2).

2 Why do you suppose Jesus attracted those rejected by polite society—such as tax collectors, prostitutes, and lepers—while other religious leaders did not?

¹¹ Jesus continued: "There was a man who had two sons. ¹² The younger one said to his father, 'Father, give me my share of the estate.' So he divided his property between them.

¹³ "Not long after that, the younger son got together all he had, set off for a distant country and there squandered his wealth in wild living. ¹⁴ After he had spent everything, there was a severe famine in that whole country, and he began to be in need. ¹⁵ So he went and hired himself out to a citizen of that country, who sent him to his fields to feed pigs. ¹⁶ He longed to fill his stomach with the pods that the pigs were eating, but no one gave him anything.

¹⁷ "When he came to his senses, he said, 'How many of my father's hired servants have food to spare, and here I am starving to death! ¹⁸ I will set out and go back to my father and say to him: Father, I have sinned against heaven and against you. ¹⁹ I am no longer worthy to be called your son; make me like one of your hired servants.' ²⁰ So he got up and went to his father.

"But while he was still a long way off, his father saw him and was filled with compassion for him; he ran to his son, threw his arms around him and kissed him.

²¹ "The son said to him, 'Father, I have sinned against heaven and against you. I am no longer worthy to be called your son.'

²² "But the father said to his servants, 'Quick! Bring the best robe and put it on him. Put a ring on his finger and sandals on his feet. ²³ Bring the fattened calf and kill it. Let's have a feast and celebrate. ²⁴ For this son of mine was dead and is alive again; he was lost and is found.' So they began to celebrate."

3 What is implied by the son's request for his share of his inheritance (v 11-12)? How would you expect the request to be received by the father?

4 Though the son gives no reason for severing all ties and moving quickly to a "distant country" outside of Jewish territory, what does verse 13 reveal about his apparent motive?

Every aspect of Jesus' story is designed to shock an orthodox Jewish audience. The son even ends up feeding pigs (v 15-16), animals which Jews considered to be unclean.

5 The text says he "came to his senses." What factors seemed to cause the son finally to change his mind and plan a return home (v 16-18)?

6 After hearing about the son's shocking betrayal of his father, what would the crowd expect the father's response to be?

7 Jesus says that "while [the son] was still a long way off" the father saw him. Try to imagine what this returning son must have looked like.

8 In verses 20-44, Jesus paints one of the most beautiful portraits of God the Father seen in the Bible. Describe what the father did and why he responded this way.

9 In this culture, for any Middle-Eastern man to run would be seen as shocking, humiliating and dishonoring, especially for a man of such dignity. Why do you suppose the father ran so urgently when he saw his son about to enter the village? How do you account for the fact that the father was watching just when the son arrived?

10 Considering his history, how do you think the son felt at receiving such lavish love from the father?

The father makes it clear that his joy and celebration is for one reason: "For this son of mine was dead and is alive again; he was lost and is found." The festivities, the robe, ring and sandals meant that the father was reinstating his son into the family and into the community. The lost son had become a full family member again. The father was offering what the son couldn't fix or solve: a new, restored relationship—only not as a master to a hired servant, but a father to a son. Now the son saw what the real issue was all along: not the money he had squandered but the relationship he had broken.

READ SOURCE TEXT: LUKE 15 V 25-32 *THE OLDER BROTHER*

"**M**eanwhile, the older son was in the field. When he came near the house, he heard music and dancing. ²⁶ So he called one of the servants and asked him what was going on. ²⁷ 'Your brother has come,' he replied, 'and your father has killed the fattened calf because he has him back safe and sound.'

²⁸ "The older brother became angry and refused to go in. So his father went out and pleaded with him. ²⁹ But he answered his father, 'Look! All these years I've been slaving for you and never disobeyed your orders. Yet you never gave me even a young goat so I could celebrate with my friends. ³⁰ But when this son of yours who has squandered your property with prostitutes comes home, you kill the fattened calf for him!'

³¹ "'My son,' the father said, 'you are always with me, and everything I have is yours. ³² But we had to celebrate and be glad, because this brother of yours was dead and is alive again; he was lost and is found.'"

But now the surprise: the older son refuses to come to the party! The father, who had run to meet his younger son, now goes out to plead with his older son to come to the party. Imagine how rude it would be if you publicly refused to come to a party hosted by a close family member!

⑪ What do you think about the reasons the older son states for his anger toward his father (v 28-30)? Though initially the son's complaints might sound reasonable, how does the father's response expose the older son's complete misperception of his father (v 31)?

⑫ For the older son, the differences between his brother and himself are all too obvious. But what are the similarities that he can't seem to see? What blocks him from seeing himself more accurately?

⑬ Most people think of sin as only behavior: a life of "sex, drugs and rock and roll." What does Jesus want these religious leaders to understand about themselves? And about the nature of God?

So, what does it mean for me?

C. S. Lewis was once asked what he believed to be unique about Christianity. He answered:

> *"Oh, that's easy. It's grace."* ("Grace" is God's undeserved love, that cannot be earned, but is freely given to all who accept his offer of it.)

How does this radical view of God's grace square with your understanding of God's attitude toward you?

Notes

4

Everybody is
Somebody
to Jesus

Everybody is Somebody to Jesus

Question

Have you ever been in a large crowd to see a famous person—a rock star, an athlete or a politician? Why do you think people flock to see famous people despite the inevitable lack of personal interaction with them?

What is it that people are seeking in our celebrity-obsessed age?

Historical context

It is springtime and Jesus is walking through Jericho on his way to Jerusalem to celebrate the Jewish festival of Passover. Jesus understands precisely what awaits him in Jerusalem. He has just told his disciples, for the third time, that he is going to die, just as the Old Testament prophets had predicted. But they fail each time to understand. They correctly believe, as did many faithful Jews, that Jesus is the long-awaited Messiah—the "anointed one" whom God had promised to send, to rescue to his people and rule them wisely and fairly. However, their view of the kingdom is short-sighted. They think Jesus will set up his kingdom on earth, free them from Roman rule and inaugurate a new era. Their expectation is that this is just about to take place during Passover (Luke 19 v 11). There is a tremendous air of excitement and huge crowds are accompanying Jesus in joyous anticipation.

It is hard to imagine what Jesus must have been thinking or feeling. Not only did his disciples still not comprehend his ultimate mission, but they didn't seem to grasp the nature and purpose of his work, as we shall see when Jesus interacts with two outcasts. One is a blind beggar and the other is a very rich, but utterly despised, tax collector.

READ SOURCE TEXT: LUKE 18 v 31-34 *JESUS PREDICTS HIS DEATH*

Jesus took the Twelve aside and told them, "We are going up to Jerusalem, and everything that is written by the prophets about the Son of Man will be fulfilled. ³² He will be delivered over to the Gentiles. They will mock him, insult him and spit on him; ³³ they will flog him and kill him. On the third day he will rise again."

³⁴ The disciples did not understand any of this. Its meaning was hidden from them, and they did not know what he was talking about.

1 Jesus is clear about what awaits him in Jerusalem and he is extremely specific with the disciples about the details of his death. Why do you think he is so resolute in his intention to walk to his death?

READ SOURCE TEXT: LUKE 18 v 35-43 *A BLIND BEGGAR*

As Jesus approached Jericho, a blind man was sitting by the roadside begging. ³⁶ When he heard the crowd going by, he asked what was happening. ³⁷ They told him, "Jesus of Nazareth is passing by."

³⁸ He called out, "Jesus, Son of David, have mercy on me!"

³⁹ Those who led the way rebuked him and told him to be quiet, but he shouted all the more, "Son of David, have mercy on me!"

⁴⁰ Jesus stopped and ordered the man to be brought to him. When he came near, Jesus asked him, ⁴¹ "What do you want me to do for you?"

"Lord, I want to see," he replied.

⁴² Jesus said to him, "Receive your sight; your faith has healed you." ⁴³ Immediately he received his sight and followed Jesus, praising God. When all the people saw it, they also praised God.

② "Those who led the way" (v 39) were no doubt the disciples. Why do you think they tried to silence the blind beggar?

③ This was a man accustomed to being marginalized. What is surprising about how he approaches Jesus (v 38-39)?

④ How is Jesus' response to the blind man a mild rebuke to his disciples (v 40)? What do you think he wanted his disciples to learn from his example?

⑤ Why do you suppose Jesus asks the beggar: "What do you want?" What internal struggle might this question have provoked in the beggar?

⑥ Jesus healed his blindness and said his faith was responsible for his healing. The blind beggar's faith in Jesus grows throughout this story. How did he demonstrate his faith in Jesus? (The phrase "Son of David" is another term for Messiah.)

The beggar gained his eyesight and a whole new productive life, and joyfully began to follow Jesus. This suggests he had become a believer. He would never have to beg again.

READ SOURCE TEXT: LUKE 19 v 1-10 *ZACCHAEUS THE TAX COLLECTOR*

Jesus entered Jericho and was passing through. ² A man was there by the name of Zacchaeus; he was a chief tax collector and was wealthy. ³ He wanted to see who Jesus was, but because he was short he could not see over the crowd. ⁴ So he ran ahead and climbed a sycamore-fig tree to see him, since Jesus was coming that way.

⁵ When Jesus reached the spot, he looked up and said to him, "Zacchaeus, come down immediately. I must stay at your house today." ⁶ So he came down at once and welcomed him gladly.

⁷ All the people saw this and began to mutter, "He has gone to be the guest of a sinner."

⁸ But Zacchaeus stood up and said to the Lord, "Look, Lord! Here and now I give half of my possessions to the poor, and if I have cheated anybody out of anything, I will pay back four times the amount."

⁹ Jesus said to him, "Today salvation has come to this house, because this man, too, is a son of Abraham. ¹⁰ For the Son of Man came to seek and to save the lost."

Jews hated Jewish tax collectors. They were seen as collaborators with imperial Rome, as they collected money for the hated Roman government. And they were extortionists who overcharged and kept a very generous amount for themselves. Tax collectors were ostracized and excluded from every part of Jewish society. That Zacchaeus is described as a chief tax collector means he was the most despised of them all!

Most people would make way in the crowd for a powerful person of great wealth. But Zacchaeus had two problems: he was short and he was hated. So he did two things that were considered humiliating for a grown man in that culture: he ran (presumably to get ahead of the crowd) and he climbed a sycamore-fig tree (v 4).

7 What do you think motivated this wealthy chief tax collector to be so desperate to see Jesus that he didn't care what others thought?

In spite of his hope of seeing Jesus while remaining unseen by the crowd, he is discovered. Jesus sees him and stops. Obviously if Jesus can see Zacchaeus, so can the crowd!

8 How do you think the crowd responded when they saw a man they intensely hated looking so vulnerable and ridiculous hiding in a tree?

9 Naturally the crowd is expecting Jesus to strongly criticize the tax collector. Instead, Jesus commands him to come down from the tree immediately and says: "I must stay at your house today." What is the crowd's response to Jesus' surprising statement (v 7)?

The crowd was not only incredulous that Jesus would go to the home of the most hated man in Jericho; they were horrified that Jesus would eat and sleep in a home they considered ceremonially unclean.

10 Zacchaeus hosts a banquet that evening. To "stand up" means he is about to make a formal announcement (v 8). What does his announcement reveal about his level of faith?

In these studies we have consistently observed people whose lives were radically transformed by confessing their sin and placing their faith in Jesus. But this is the first time we are given a glimpse into the transformation that faith makes in the life of a new believer.

⑪ How does the costly love that Jesus demonstrated to Zacchaeus affect how he chose to live out his faith before others?

⑫ Zacchaeus had clearly not found meaning in his pursuit of wealth. But because of his shady past, he couldn't have imagined ever being accepted by someone like Jesus. How do you think he felt as he heard Jesus say the words in verse 9?

Jesus summarized his ministry like this: "For the Son of Man came to seek and to save the lost."

⑬ What qualities did the blind beggar and Zacchaeus have in common that allowed them to be "found" by Jesus?

So, what could this mean for us?

Zacchaeus and the blind beggar didn't realize it, but that day in Jericho was their last chance! Jesus would die on a cross in a matter of days, exactly as he had predicted. What this story conveys is that God offers his love to the poor and to the rich, to the oppressed and even to the oppressor! The issue isn't whether God reaches out to us—it's whether we choose to respond to him. He will not violate our will—the choice is ours.

In light of what we have learned about God's love for us, why do you think some choose to resist a God like this?

Notes

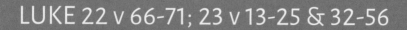

5

Game Over?

Question

In twentieth-century Western societies, it was widely believed that human nature was fundamentally good, that evil was largely caused by ignorance and bad housing, and that education and social reform would enable us to live together in happiness and good will. And yet the 20th century was one of the bloodiest of any in human history.

What evidence do you see that this prior optimism was unrealistic?

Historical context

During this series we have seen Jesus seek and find the lost as he offers healing, love and forgiveness. We have learned that while grace is beautiful, it isn't cheap. For Jesus it always involved a cost. Now we will see the ultimate price Jesus was willing to pay in order to win us back.

Much has happened to Jesus by the time this passage begins. Jesus and his disciples have just spent the night in the Garden of Gethsemane, where Jesus experienced deep personal agony, knowing what he was about to face. While they were still in the garden, the Roman guards, along with the religious leaders and the disciple who betrayed him, Judas, came to arrest Jesus. Through the night and very early morning there were four sets of interrogations. Jesus suffered severe beatings, vicious mockery, a public lashing, and the knowledge that all of his disciples had fled in fear. Peter would deny three times that he even knew him, just as Jesus had predicted. All of this took place before he was nailed to the cross at nine o'clock in the morning.

At daybreak the council of the elders of the people, both the chief priests and the teachers of the law, met together, and Jesus was led before them. 67 "If you are the Messiah," they said, "tell us."

Jesus answered, "If I tell you, you will not believe me, 68 and if I asked you, you would not answer. 69 But from now on, the Son of Man will be seated at the right hand of the mighty God."

70 They all asked, "Are you then the Son of God?"

He replied, "You say that I am."

71 Then they said, "Why do we need any more testimony? We have heard it from his own lips."

1 When the Jewish religious leaders gathered, for what claim of Jesus did they agree to have him killed (v 67-71)?

Upon completing their interrogation very early on Friday morning, the Jewish leaders rush Jesus to the palace of the Roman governor, Pontius Pilate (under Roman rule the Jews had no authority to carry out the death penalty). They falsely charge Jesus with treason against Rome before Pilate in order to obtain the death penalty. Pilate interrogates Jesus and finds him innocent. Pilate knows that the religious leaders have no case. Three times he tells the increasingly riotous crowd that Jesus is innocent.

READ SOURCE TEXT: LUKE 23 v 13-25 *PILATE'S RESPONSE*

Pilate called together the chief priests, the rulers and the people, 14 and said to them, "You brought me this man as one who was inciting the people to rebellion. I have examined him in your presence and have found no basis for your charges against him. 15 Neither has Herod, for he sent him back to us; as you can see, he has done nothing to deserve death. ¹⁶ Therefore, I will punish him and then release him." [¹⁷ At every Passover Festival Pilate had to set free one prisoner for them.]

¹⁸ But the whole crowd shouted, "Away with this man! Release Barabbas to us!" ¹⁹ (Barabbas had been thrown into prison for an insurrection in the city, and for murder.)

²⁰ Wanting to release Jesus, Pilate appealed to them again. ²¹ But they kept shouting, "Crucify him! Crucify him!"

²² For the third time he spoke to them: "Why? What crime has this man committed? I have found in him no grounds for the death penalty. Therefore I will have him punished and then release him."

²³ But with loud shouts they insistently demanded that he be crucified, and their shouts prevailed. ²⁴ So Pilate decided to grant their demand. ²⁵ He released the man who had been thrown into prison for insurrection and murder, the one they asked for, and surrendered Jesus to their will.

2 Why did Pilate finally give in to the Jewish leaders (v 23-25)?

READ SOURCE TEXT: LUKE 23 v 32-43 *THE CRUCIFIXION*

Two other men, both criminals, were also led out with him to be executed. ³³ When they came to the place called the Skull, they crucified him there, along with the criminals—one on his right, the other on his left. ³⁴ Jesus said, "Father, forgive them, for they do not know what they are doing." And they divided up his clothes by casting lots.

³⁵ The people stood watching, and the rulers even sneered at him. They said, "He saved others; let him save himself if he is God's Messiah, the Chosen One."

³⁶ The soldiers also came up and mocked him. They offered him wine vinegar ³⁷ and said, "If you are the king of the Jews, save yourself."

³⁸ There was a written notice above him, which read: THIS IS THE KING OF THE JEWS.

³⁹ One of the criminals who hung there hurled insults at him: "Aren't you the Messiah? Save yourself and us!"

⁴⁰ But the other criminal rebuked him. "Don't you fear God," he said, "since you are under the same sentence? ⁴¹ We are punished justly, for we are getting what our deeds deserve. But this man has done nothing wrong."

⁴² Then he said, "Jesus, remember me when you come into your kingdom."

⁴³ Jesus answered him, "Truly I tell you, today you will be with me in paradise."

According to Cicero (106-43 BC), crucifixion was "the worst and cruelest" form of torture. It was designed to be the most humiliating and gruesome method of execution. It was reserved for the worst offenders. It usually ended in a horrible death by shock or asphyxiation.

3 Once Jesus and the two criminals arrive at the place where they will be crucified, what is Jesus' response to the Roman soldiers' callous behavior (v 34)? What might the criminals have thought upon hearing this?

4 Describe the conversation between the two criminals and what is revealed about each of them as they face certain death (v 39-41)? What remarkable request does the second criminal make of Jesus (v 42)?

5 What does it tell us about Jesus that in his final hours he focuses on saving others rather than himself (v 43)?

READ SOURCE TEXT: LUKE 23 v 44-56 *THE DEATH OF JESUS*

It was now about noon, and darkness came over the whole land until three in the afternoon, ⁴⁵ for the sun stopped shining. And the curtain of the temple was torn in two. ⁴⁶ Jesus called out with a loud voice, "Father, into your hands I commit my spirit." When he had said this, he breathed his last.

⁴⁷ The centurion, seeing what had happened, praised God and said, "Surely this was a righteous man." ⁴⁸ When all the people who

had gathered to witness this sight saw what took place, they beat their breasts and went away. [49] But all those who knew him, including the women who had followed him from Galilee, stood at a distance, watching these things.

[50] Now there was a man named Joseph, a member of the Council, a good and upright man, [51] who had not consented to their decision and action. He came from the Judean town of Arimathea, and he himself was waiting for the kingdom of God. [52] Going to Pilate, he asked for Jesus' body. [53] Then he took it down, wrapped it in linen cloth and placed it in a tomb cut in the rock, one in which no one had yet been laid. [54] It was Preparation Day, and the Sabbath was about to begin.

[55] The women who had come with Jesus from Galilee followed Joseph and saw the tomb and how his body was laid in it. [56] Then they went home and prepared spices and perfumes. But they rested on the Sabbath in obedience to the commandment.

6 Jesus was put on the cross about 9 am. What strange thing occurred between noon and 3 pm?

This wasn't a solar eclipse, which lasts only a few minutes—this went on for three hours. The darkness was supernatural. It was a sign of God's judgment. But the judgment for our sins fell on Jesus instead of us, just as the Bible reveals:

> God made him who had no sin to be sin for us, so that in him we might become the righteousness of God. (2 Corinthians 5 v 21)

> God demonstrates his own love for us in this: While we were still sinners, Christ died for us. (Romans 5 v 8)

7 For someone in Jesus' physical condition on the cross, it would be nearly impossible to speak. Why is it significant that Jesus cried out in a loud voice and said: "Father, into your hands I commit my spirit"?

Then another amazing thing happens. At the heart of the Jewish temple was a smaller temple called the Most Holy Place, where God symbolically dwelt. Because God is holy and pure, there was a curtain that separated sinful people from God's presence. The curtain was six inches thick, as substantial as a wall.

8. As Jesus died, the massive curtain was ripped open. We are told in another Gospel that the tear was from the top to the bottom (just to make clear who had done it!). What do you think it signified that the curtain was ripped open? What had Jesus' death made possible?

9. The centurion was a hardened Roman executioner who had seen countless people die over the years. Yet Luke tells us, in verse 47, that at the moment of Jesus' death, he praised God and declared Jesus righteous (sinless). In Mark's Gospel we are told he also said: "Surely this man was the Son of God!" (Mark 15 v 39) What did he see that led him to think that Jesus was not just a man, but also divine?

So, what does it mean for us?

Thoughtful people have noted that there are two central questions in life: what is the essence of our problem, and what is the solution?

What is the problem? John Stott, a Christian author, put it this way: *"The essence of sin is substituting ourselves for God."* What is the solution? Stott continued: *"The essence of salvation is God substituting himself for us."*

Bono, the lead singer of the rock group U2, said in a magazine interview:

> *"At the centre of all religions is the idea of karma: you know, an eye for an eye—every action is met by an equal or an opposite one. And then along comes this idea of grace. God's grace can interrupt the stupid mess we've made of all our lives... If karma is my final judge, then I'm in big trouble because I've done such stupid stuff. If it's our goodness that decided our fate, then we're all in trouble... Grace doesn't excuse my mistakes, but I'm holding out that Jesus took my sins and the sins of the whole world onto the cross. We don't deserve it, but it's what enables us to start over. It's what gives us hope."*

The message of *karma* says: "You sin—you pay." But the message of the gospel says: "You sin—and God pays."

From everything you have learned about Jesus thus far, do you think Bono is right that Jesus is the one who can enable us to start over?

Notes

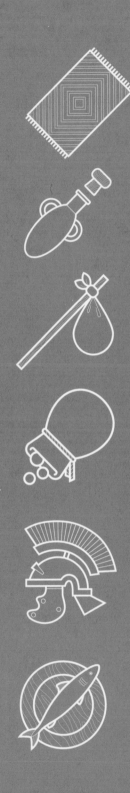

6

The Son Also Rises!

Question

Can humans live a satisfied life without hope?

In the film *The Shawshank Redemption*, Andy, a banker who has been imprisoned for a double murder he did not commit, tells Red, a man he befriends in prison: "Fear can hold you prisoner. Hope can set you free." Why is hope dangerous if it isn't founded in truth?

Historical context

Try to imagine how the disciples felt in the days immediately following Jesus' death. Their hopes were dashed. What questions might they have asked? *Why did Jesus insist on dying? Why didn't he escape when he had the chance? What are we to do now?*

Immediately following Jesus' death, his body was wrapped and sealed in a tomb. The Romans rolled a heavy stone (that would have required many men to move) to cover the opening of the tomb. They ordered battle-hardened soldiers to guard the tomb to ensure there would be no tampering.

But on the third day an event happened that changed everything. First, the women reported to the disciples that not only had they found the tomb empty, but Mary Magdalene had seen the risen Lord! The disciples rejected their report out of hand: "They did not believe the women, because their words seemed to them like nonsense" (Luke 24 v 11). But over the next 40 days, seven appearances are recounted in the four Gospels. The apostle Paul wrote that five hundred people saw him in one "sighting" and he added: "Most of [them] are still living" (1 Corinthians 15 v 6). In other words: *Check it out yourselves; don't just rely on my report!*

The Roman government and the Jewish leaders were desperate. They turned Jerusalem upside down trying to find Jesus' corpse. That was all they needed to prove that it was a hoax. Yet the body was never found. So they concocted a story: "His disciples came during the night and stole him away while we were asleep" (Matthew 28 v 12-15). Yet how were sleeping men able to identify who stole the body?

We will read about one resurrection appearance that occurred late Sunday on the third day. Two followers of Jesus have rushed back to Jerusalem from their village in Emmaus to tell the disciples they have just seen Jesus alive.

READ SOURCE TEXT: LUKE 24 v 36-49 *JESUS AND HIS FRIENDS*

While they were still talking about this, Jesus himself stood among them and said to them, "Peace be with you."

³⁷ They were startled and frightened, thinking they saw a ghost. ³⁸ He said to them, "Why are you troubled, and why do doubts rise in your minds? ³⁹ Look at my hands and my feet. It is I myself! Touch me and see; a ghost does not have flesh and bones, as you see I have."

⁴⁰ When he had said this, he showed them his hands and feet. ⁴¹ And while they still did not believe it because of joy and amazement, he asked them, "Do you have anything here to eat?" ⁴² They gave him a piece of broiled fish, ⁴³ and he took it and ate it in their presence.

⁴⁴ He said to them, "This is what I told you while I was still with you: Everything must be fulfilled that is written about me in the Law of Moses, the Prophets and the Psalms."

⁴⁵ Then he opened their minds so they could understand the Scriptures. ⁴⁶ He told them, "This is what is written: The Messiah will suffer and rise from the dead on the third day, ⁴⁷ and repentance for the forgiveness of sins will be preached in his name to all nations, be-

ginning at Jerusalem. ⁴⁸ You are witnesses of these things. ⁴⁹ I am going to send you what my Father has promised; but stay in the city until you have been clothed with power from on high."

1. We often assume that people in the 1st century were easily convinced of spiritual realities, unlike our more cynical age. Jesus repeatedly told his disciples: "I will die, but I'll rise on the third day." It is now the third day. What is their reaction when Jesus appears before them (v 37-38)?

2. Why do you think they are terrified that they are seeing a ghost? Does their reaction strike you as people prone to being easily fooled?

3. What evidence does Jesus give them that it is truly him? What is significant about showing them his hands and feet?

4. Imagine you are in a room with the disciples. What thoughts and emotions would be going through your mind? What does it mean that they "did not believe it because of joy"?

5. What further request does Jesus make and why (v 41)? In a little while Jesus would leave, but what might be additional proof that he had truly been with them?

6. Why do you think Jesus didn't appeal to their emotions but instead kept appealing to their senses?

7. For the disciples, it was incomprehensible that the Messiah and Savior would die such a humiliating and shameful death. What crucial information does Jesus remind them of (v 44-45)?

8. Clearly, it was very important to Jesus that the disciples understood what they had witnessed at the cross. What two events had been prophesied throughout the whole of the Old Testament that the Messiah would do (v 46)?

9. In Luke's Gospel we have seen how God, through Christ, reaches out in love and offers his grace to one and all. We have also seen that two responses are necessary if we are to receive his grace. The first is placing our faith in Christ. What is the second response, mentioned in verse 47? Why is our willingness to admit fault so important in any significant relationship?

⑩ When we respond in faith and repentance, God receives us gladly and offers us two gifts. What is the first gift mentioned in verse 47? Why is it so necessary in any relationship of intimacy?

The second gift is the promise of the Holy Spirit, which Jesus promises to give the disciples once he returns to heaven (that story is recorded in Acts 1). All believers are given the gift of God's Spirit, who dwells in us and empowers us to become the people we were meant to be.

⑪ From that point on, the disciples became bold and courageous in proclaiming the good news of Jesus. Tradition says that nearly all the disciples died as martyrs. What do you suppose transformed them from being fearful men into becoming bold, courageous witnesses ready to die for their faith?

So, what does this mean for us?

In *The Shawshank Redemption*, Andy is initially shattered by the realization that human evil is a profound reality: from discovering his wife's infidelity to being falsely imprisoned. He is then enlisted by a publicly devout but privately corrupt prison warden who demands his help in laundering money. What is Andy's solution to the corruption he sees everywhere? He devises a brilliant but devious plan to take the warden's dirty money for himself after he escapes from prison.

But can the reality of evil be solved by human cleverness? Or even by physical force? When Peter saw Jesus being arrested in Gethsemane, he drew out his sword to fight. But Jesus told him to put his sword away. The problem of evil cannot ultimately be solved by political subversion and armed conflict any more than by Andy's ingenious but unethical plan.

The Bible says that Jesus, God's Son, came from heaven to pay the penalty for our sins. That is why the resurrection is so important. The resurrection offers proof that God's way of covering our debt has been accomplished, once and for all, through the cross. Jesus' scars are therefore tremendously significant.

Think of it—only the Christian God bears scars. When the disciples first saw those nails go into Jesus' hands and feet, they though it meant the end of their dreams; their cause was over. Only when they saw Jesus alive again, bearing those scars, did they realize that his wounds hadn't ruined their lives as they had thought—now they understood that the ancient prophecy in Isaiah, written some 700 years before Jesus was even born, had finally been fulfilled:

> *But he was pierced for our transgressions, he was crushed for our iniquities; the punishment that brought us peace was upon him, and by his wounds we are healed. We all, like sheep, have gone astray, each of us has turned to our own way; and the Lord has laid on him the iniquity of us all. (Isaiah 53 v 5-6)*

Suppose you witnessed the crucifixion of Jesus. Then suppose the risen Lord appeared to you, just as he did to his disciples. What do you think he would say to you? How would you respond?

Notes

thegoodbook
COMPANY

Opening up the Bible

Thanks for reading this book. We hope you enjoyed it, and found it helpful.

Most people want to find answers to the big questions of life: Who are we? Why are we here? How should we live? But for many valid reasons we are often unable to find the time or the right space to think positively and carefully about them.

Perhaps you have questions that you need an answer for. Perhaps you have met Christians who have seemed unsympathetic or incomprehensible. Or maybe you are someone who has grown up believing, but need help to make things a little clearer.

At The Good Book Company, we're passionate about producing materials that help people of all ages and stages understand the heart of the Christian message, which is found in the pages of the Bible.

Whoever you are, and wherever you are at when it comes to these big questions, we hope we can help. As a publisher we want to help you look at the good book that is the Bible because we're convinced that as we meet the person who stands at its centre—Jesus Christ—we find the clearest answers to our biggest questions.

Visit our website to discover the range of books, videos and other resources we produce, or visit our partner site www.christianityexplored.org for a clear explanation of who Jesus is and why he came.

Thanks again for reading,

Your friends at The Good Book Company

UK & EUROPE	thegoodbook.co.uk	0333 123 0880
NORTH AMERICA	thegoodbook.com	866 244 2165
AUSTRALIA	thegoodbook.com.au	(02) 9564 3555
NEW ZEALAND	thegoodbook.co.nz	(+64) 3 343 2463

 WWW.CHRISTIANITYEXPLORED.ORG
Our partner site is a great place for those exploring the Christian faith, with a clear explanation of the good news, powerful testimonies and answers to difficult questions.